SCRIPTURES *for the*
ADVENT SEASON

MEETING THE

MESSIAH

with LEADER'S GUIDE

KARA LASSEN OLIVER

UPPER
ROOM BOOKS®
NASHVILLE

Cover design: Bruce DeRoos/Left Coast Design
Cover image: "Mother and Child" by J. Kirk Richards
        www.jkirkrichards.com
Interior Layout: Nancy Terzian/Buckinghorse Design
        www.buckinghorsedesign.com
First printing: 2010

ISBN 978-0-8358-1029-6
Printed in the United States of America

CONTENTS

Welcome   5

Reading Scripture Devotionally   10

Informational Reading and Formational Reading   16

WEEK 1   The Holy Spirit   19

WEEK 2   John the Baptist   31

WEEK 3   Mary   43

WEEK 4   The Shepherds   55

WEEK 5   Jesus   67

WEEK 6   The Magi   79

Leader's Guide   91

Notes   127

WELCOME

Welcome to *Meeting the Messiah: Scriptures for the Advent Season*. Advent (from the Latin word *adventus*, meaning "arrival " and *ad* + *venire*, "to come to") is a season of the Christian year, the period of expectant waiting and preparation for the celebration of the birth of Jesus. While the children in our families and in our congregations understand the "expectation" of Christmas Day, many of us have forgotten this expectant waiting. The waiting we associate with Christmas is waiting in lines, waiting for packages to arrive, waiting for cookies to bake, and waiting for family to decide who will host Christmas dinner and who will bring the pies.

Our Christian tradition and our local churches provide rituals and ceremonies that aim to slow us down in order to appreciate and recognize the importance of this season—Chrismon trees, children's pageants, Christmas concerts, and international celebrations like Las Posadas. But often our daily thoughts and activities during the season are pushed and pulled toward the more secular tasks, parties, and, frankly, stresses.

In the midst of all that calls to you in this season, you have chosen to attend to your spiritual life, to the spirit of

Advent. You have chosen a countercultural path—to set time apart to pray and listen and to wait expectantly for arrival of the Christ child—when you could be spending those same hours scanning the ads in the paper or hanging more lights at the windows, just hoping Jesus' birthday would hurry up and get here.

So, welcome! Welcome to the waiting, welcome to the anticipation, welcome to this journey of prophecies fulfilled, divine visitations, faith and obedience, choirs of angels, unexpected guests, and precious gifts.

THE JOURNEY

Meeting the Messiah hopes to provide an opportunity for you to journey through Advent at a different pace and with a purposeful focus on the Christ child, whether by yourself or with a small group of fellow pilgrims. Over the next six weeks, you're invited to explore the stories of Advent, Christmas, and Epiphany from the vantage point of the Holy Spirit, John the Baptist, Mary, the shepherds, Jesus, and the Magi. As you read, pray, and journal, you will have the opportunity to put yourself in the place of those who first prepared for and encountered the Messiah. Interruptions to daily life, surprises, setting plans aside—all come into play.

In the midst of our plans, our to-do lists, and our daily life, we will seek wisdom and insight about how to respond to God who is with us, to prepare for Jesus' coming, to celebrate, worship, and offer our best gifts to the Christ child. How will we meet the Messiah this year?

.

DAILY STEPS

The scriptures chosen for the daily readings loosely follow the lectionary, a program for Bible reading arranged in a three-year cycle. So some scripture passages may not directly refer to the biblical figure highlighted that week, but they will touch on motivation, action, or feelings related to that particular figure in the context of the coming of the Messiah. For example, in the final week, The Magi, not all passages are about the Magi. The week coincides with Epiphany Sunday, when the church celebrates its mission to the world in light of Jesus' birth; that theme is linked to the visit of the Magi.

As you read each day's entry, you will be guided to respond personally to short scripture passages. Space is provided for you to write about your responses. Reflecting and journaling in this way will take you deeper into the stories.

You will read thirty passages, one per day for five days during each of the next six weeks. For each reading, an *entry point*, a phrase or statement that focuses on a few verses from the day's passage, suggests a way to explore the scripture's message personally. The daily readings and entry-point activities will facilitate reflection on your interests, preferences, gifts, and talents. These activities will require no more than ten to fifteen minutes daily.

If you choose to use this book in a group setting, at the end of each week, you will gather with others to reflect on the week's readings and entry points. A Leader's Guide for conducting small-group sessions is part of this book.

One entry point each week is marked with two stars (**). If you're unable to do all the readings and responses in a week, try to find time to do this one; it will be used in some way during the weekly group meeting. No other preparation for the group meeting is necessary (unless you are the leader). Bring this book and a Bible with you to the group meetings.

THE VALUE OF A SPIRITUAL JOURNAL

Meeting the Messiah offers you a chance to try journaling during the Advent season. Keeping a personal journal is a Christian practice that helps you attend to God's presence and work in daily life and events. What you write here is private—just between you and God. If you participate in a small group with *Meeting the Messiah*, you will take your book to group meetings, but you will never be asked to reveal the contents of your journaling to others. You take your book to remind yourself of reflections during the past week and to record responses to some of the group activities.

Anything you choose to record in your journal entries is fine. This book is yours! You may write a prayer in response to a scripture reading. You may draw a picture of an image the reading brings to mind, or you may make note of an idea or insight you want to remember. You may write about connections you sense between the Bible's words and your life. If you need help getting started, here are some questions you can use to journal in response to the scripture readings:

- What picture of God do I see in this passage?
- What does this passage tell me about human nature?
- What does this passage reveal about God's ways of relating to us?
- What connection do I sense between this passage and my life right now?

- What feelings and memories arise as I reflect on this passage?
- What questions does this passage raise for me?
- How does this passage suggest that I might pray?
- What other response does this passage ask of me?

If you're a first-time journaler, don't think of this as a task that must be done every day or something to worry about doing correctly. The value of a spiritual journal is that it helps you pay attention to God. It is not an end in itself.

Start with a few words or phrases. Record your thoughts and feelings even if they seem irrelevant or off topic. We trust that God is revealed anew in each reading of scripture. The message for you may be radically different than for your spouse, friend, or classmates, but you can trust that in the prayer and silence, God has a word for you. Recording these thoughts and insights throughout a week—those that make sense and those that seem like tangents—may become a clear message or insight over the course of the days and weeks. Be patient with yourself and with God, journaling your thoughts and prayers.

READING SCRIPTURE DEVOTIONALLY

by M. Robert Mulholland Jr.

The moment we open a book, a powerful set of habitual practices begins to work. Our culture teaches us learning methods that establish the reader as the controlling power who seeks to master the text in order to use it for his or her own purposes. The cognitive, analytical aspects of our beings are hyperdeveloped in our culture; we tend to think that the sharper we are intellectually, the smarter we are, the more quickly we grasp concepts and synthesize them, the more balanced we are.

Responding to God with our whole being entails loving God with all of our mind and using our cognitive abilities. We cannot shirk this aspect. Jesus, however, puts loving God with the heart and soul higher on his list: "'Love the Lord your God with all your heart and with all your soul and with all your mind'" (Matt. 22:37). Loving God with heart and soul precedes loving God with mind. Listing *mind* last doesn't make it less important but implies that it is not the only way to respond to God—or even the dominant way to respond, as our culture asserts. (All three synoptic Gospels [see Mark 12:30; Luke 10:27] employ the same order.)

Our culture's predominant mode of response, however, is often the rational, cognitive, and intellectual. When this mind-set becomes our only mode of reading scripture, we may find it difficult to have "ears to hear" (Mark 4:9, 23; Luke 8:8; 14:35). When the mind is our primary filter for scripture, our approach can create an imbalance. We can easily read scripture in a purely cognitive way and decide that this passage doesn't apply to us. (We frequently even pick out some other troublesome person who should obviously heed this text instead of ourselves!) This purely cognitive way of reading insulates the "door" of our being against God's "knocking." Why? We are not really opening our being at deeper levels to the possibility of meeting God in that passage.

What if God wishes to meet us in the passage in an intimate way, according to God's wisdom, communicating what we need to hear but wish to avoid? Allowing God's Word to speak transformationally to the deepest levels of our being invites us to develop another way of reading.

FORMATIONAL SCRIPTURE READING

Formational scripture reading differs from our usual approach. Formational scripture reading invites us to open ourselves, allowing God to set the agenda for our lives through the text. It facilitates genuine spiritual formation—the process of being conformed to the image of Jesus Christ. Reading formationally helps us open our "rational filter," which can sift out so much of God's voice. We begin to hear at the heart-and-soul level. Jesus frequently reminded people of the importance of having "ears to hear" (Mark 4:9, 23; Luke 8:8; 14:35).

Formational reading can help us develop those ears to hear. Let me share a personal experience of formational reading. I was following a prescribed plan for Bible reading and had come to the Exodus event. I'd read about the struggle between God and Pharaoh many times but only informationally. As I read the daily assigned portion, I sat before it and said, *Lord, what are you seeking to say to me through this?* All sorts of thoughts went through my mind—who said what, Pharaoh's resistance, God's hardening Pharaoh's heart. I got nothing from the text after wrestling with it for a week or more. Finally, each day's portion moved one by one through the ten plagues. I was met each time with silence—or my own noisy understanding of the passage. As I moved toward the end of the passage about the plagues and asked that same question, an answer came: *You are Pharaoh! What?* I replied. *Me, Pharaoh? Moses, perhaps, even one of the Hebrews, but Pharaoh? Perhaps a servant or slave, but Pharaoh?* Possibilities began to open up in the text and inside me. I realized that God had given me certain gifts, abilities, and personality traits. All these were God's "children," but I had enslaved them to my own purposes, desires, intentions, and plans. Truly I was the Pharaoh of my life! I came to the last plague—the death of the firstborn. I saw that for me to cease to be Pharaoh in my life, there had to be a death of my "firstborn" desires to use God's gifts for my own purposes. To liberate those gifts for God's use in my life, I would have to cease to be Pharaoh.

CHARACTERISTICS OF FORMATIONAL SCRIPTURE READING

Depth. Informational reading seeks to cover as much material as possible as quickly as possible, while formational reading involves smaller portions of scripture. The point is not just to get through the text but to become personally involved in it. Formational reading is concerned with depth, so we may find ourselves "holding on" to just one sentence or paragraph or page for quite a while. We allow the passage to open out to us its deeper dynamics and multiple layers of meaning. *We let the text intrude into our life and address us.*

Openness. In formational reading, *we let the text master us.* We come to the text with an openness to hear, to receive, and to respond. This may feel risky because it lays us open to unforeseen conclusions.

Humility. Formational reading requires a humble approach, a new inner posture in which we willingly relinquish our insights and purposes. We stand before scripture and await its address.

Mystery. Informational reading can be characterized by a problem-solving mentality. When we do respond, we often read our needs and desires into the scripture, asking, *Does this passage solve my problems, answer my questions, meet my needs?* Formational reading invites us to become open to the whole mystery of God. We allow God to address us however God wishes. Eventually, we may discover that problem-solving dynamics emerge from the encounter, but we relinquish the right to solve our problems with scripture.

SUGGESTIONS FOR FORMATIONAL
SCRIPTURE READING

Make listening for God's voice a top priority. Focus your attention on what God is saying to you as you read. Listen for God to speak to you in and through, around and within, over and behind the words. Keep asking yourself, *What is God seeking to say to me in all of this?* Allow the text to become an instrument of God's voice in your life. Respond to what you read with your heart and spirit.

Let your response take place down in the deeper levels of your being. Ask yourself questions such as: *How do I feel about what is being said? How am I reacting? How am I responding down deep within myself? What is going on inside of me?* Then begin to ask yourself "why" questions: *Why do I feel this way? Why am I responding in this manner? Why do I have these feelings within?*

Let this exercise be *an opportunity to get in touch with the deeper layers of your being.* What do your reactions tell you about your habits, your attitudes, your perspectives, your responses, and your reactions to life? Are you beginning to see something about yourself? Thomas à Kempis said, "A humble knowledge of ourselves is a surer way to God than is the search for depth of learning." That humble knowledge of yourself can come when you read scripture if you balance your cognitive response pattern with this affective response from deep within your being.

Prepare to read by quieting yourself. You can't run in, sit down, pick up the text, and read scripture formationally. You have to "center down," to use the old Quaker phrase—*become still, relinquish your agenda, and acknowledge the presence of*

God. You may have to relax first in order to do this. When you center yourself in this way, you may find that no word addresses you out of that text on that day, but the constant discipline of preparing yourself and entering into formational reading will itself be spiritually forming to your soul.

Allow the two kinds of reading—informational and formational—to work together. You may begin reading a scripture passage with informational dynamics, but then you must be sensitive to the need to move to the formational dynamics of reading. Allow yourself to become open and receptive to the intrusion of the living Word of God into your garbled, distorted self. You may get tripped up on an informational point and need to move back to an informational mode. There is a necessary interplay between these two approaches, but *you'll ultimately need to arrive at a disciplined development of the formational mode of approaching the text.* As we become skilled at shifting to that inner posture of becoming listeners, we develop "ears to hear." We become receptive and accessible to being addressed by the living Word of God.

M. Robert Mulholland Jr. is professor emeritus of New Testament at Asbury Theological Seminary where he taught for thirty-one years and is a retired elder in the Kentucky Annual Conference of the United Methodist Church. He is author of *Shaped by the Word* (Upper Room Books), *The Deeper Journey* (InterVarsity Press), and *The Way of Scripture* (Upper Room Books), among other publications.

INFORMATIONAL AND FORMATIONAL READING

Reading for information is an integral part of teaching and learning. But reading is also concerned with listening for the special guidance, for the particular insight, for your relationship with God. What matters is the attitude of the mind and heart.

INFORMATIONAL READING

1. Informational reading is concerned with covering as much material as possible and as quickly as possible.

2. Informational reading is linear—seeking an objective meaning, truth, or principle to apply.

3. Informational reading seeks to master the text.

4. In informational reading, the text is an object out there for us to control.

5. Informational reading is analytical, critical, and judgmental.

6. Informational reading is concerned with problem solving.

Adapted from content in *Shaped by the Word: The Power of Scripture in Spiritual Formation*, rev. ed., by M. Robert Mulholland Jr. (Nashville, TN: Upper Room Books, 2000), 49–63. Used by permission of Upper Room Books.

FORMATIONAL READING

1. Formational reading is concerned with small portions of content rather than quantity.

2. Formational reading focuses on depth and seeks multiple layers of meaning in a single passage.

3. Formational reading allows the text to master the student.

4. Formational reading sees the student as the object to be shaped by the text.

5. Formational reading requires a humble, detached, willing, loving approach.

6. Formational reading is open to mystery. Students come to the scripture to stand before the Mystery called God and to let the Mystery address them.

OBSTACLES TO HEARING GOD IN SCRIPTURE

- thinking/talking about scripture

- classifying

- comparing

- describing

- explaining

- looking for "the lesson" rather than listening to scripture:
    the actual words that are there
    the emotions we feel
    the connections we make
    the memories that arise

THE HOLY SPIRIT

The Holy Spirit proceeds, inspires, and motivates all that is enfolded in the Christmas story. Unbidden and beyond human control, the Spirit of God moves through history, giving visions to the prophets of old, drawing attention to injustice, and warning believers to return to the covenant with God. We cannot predict the coming of the Spirit or its mode or method of arrival. But we can learn to pay attention, to seek and listen for the gentle whisper or booming voice of the Holy's Spirit's presence.

As we enter into this Advent season, the Holy Spirit will be trying to break into our lives, prompting us to remember the child behind our toy donations, nudging us to see the injustice of society that creates the need for soup kitchens where we volunteer, warning us in the midst of family gatherings to remember our covenant of love and faithfulness made with a spouse or partner, and calling us to actually hear and live the words of glad tidings in the Christmas hymns that will surround us in our cars, homes, and shopping malls.

Take time to welcome and cherish silence in the midst of this busy season. In these quiet times of prayer and conversation with God, hear the Holy Spirit calling to you. As you prepare to meet the Messiah, this awareness will enhance your ability to recognize and respond to the Spirit.

DAY 1

Entry Point

A Messenger Comes in Many Ways

READ MALACHI 3:1-4.

Read again Malachi 3:1-2. See, I am sending my messenger to prepare the way before me, and the Lord whom you seek will suddenly come to his temple. The messenger of the covenant in whom you delight—indeed, he is coming, says the LORD of hosts. But who can endure the day of his coming, and who can stand when he appears? For he is like a refiner's fire and like fullers' soap.

Saint Teresa of Ávila (1515–1582) was a Spanish mystic, Carmelite nun, and writer. In her book *The Interior Castle*, she explores ways a soul is gradually transformed into the likeness of God.

> [God's] appeals come through the conversations of good people, or from sermons, or through the reading of good books; and there are many other ways . . . in which God calls us. Or they come through sicknesses and trials, or by means of truths which God teaches us at times when we are engaged in prayer; however feeble such prayers may be, God values them highly. You must not despise this first favour, . . . nor be disconsolate, even though you have not responded immediately to the Lord's call; for His Majesty is quite prepared to wait for many days, and even years, especially when He sees we are persevering and have good desires.[1]

Think about various ways that the Holy Spirit, God's messenger, has come to you in your life. Journal here about those memories. As you enter into this Advent study, choose a time and space for your daily devotions, making room for the Holy Spirit to prepare you for Advent.

DAY 2

Entry Point
**This City

READ JEREMIAH 33:10-16.

Read again Jeremiah 33:10-11. Thus says the LORD: In this place of which you say, "It is a waste without human beings or animals," in the towns of Judah and the streets of Jerusalem that are desolate, without inhabitants, human or animal, there shall once more be heard the voice of mirth and the voice of gladness, the voice of the bridegroom and the voice of the bride, the voices of those who sing, as they bring thank offerings to the house of the LORD: "Give thanks to the LORD of hosts, for the LORD is good, for his steadfast love endures forever!" For I will restore the fortunes of the land as at first, says the LORD.

Talk with a companion (or dialogue with God) about the ways in which your community could be described as a "waste" (v. 10). In what way are justice and righteousness needed? What needs to be "saved," and what issues of safety need to be addressed? Sit in a public place and observe the people and animals. What are they doing? What can you learn about them by just watching them? What spirit can you feel in your community today? As you watch and question, silently invite both the people and the animals to "Give thanks to the LORD of hosts, for the LORD is good; for his steadfast love endures forever!"

Reflect on your observations of people and animals, and then journal here about that experience.

DAY 3

Entry Point
Pay Attention to Today!

READ LUKE 21:25-36.

Read again Luke 21:34-36. Be on guard so that your hearts are not weighed down with dissipation and drunkenness and the worries of this life, and that day catch you unexpectedly, like a trap. For it will come upon all who live on the face of the whole earth. Be alert at all times, praying that you may have the strength to escape all these things that will take place, and to stand before the Son of Man.

Jesus warns about preoccupation with end-times predictions (21:8) and instead commands simple attentiveness to God's presence every moment of every day: "Be alert at all times" (21:36).

How can you nurture what Jean-Pierre de Caussade called "the sacrament of the present moment"? He described it this way: "This discovery of divine action in everything that happens, each moment, is the most subtle wisdom possible regarding the ways of God in this life."[2] What practices help you cultivate this simple attentiveness?

DAY 4

Entry Point
God's Shining Face

Read Psalm 80:1-19.

Read again Psalm 80:7-13.

> Restore us, O God of hosts;
>> let your face shine, that we may be saved.
> You brought a vine out of Egypt;
>> you drove out the nations and planted it.
> You cleared the ground for it;
>> it took deep root and filled the land.
> The mountains were covered with its shade,
>> the mighty cedars with its branches;
> it sent out its branches to the sea,
>> and its shoots to the River.
> Why then have you broken down its walls,
>> so that all who pass along the way pluck its fruit?
> The boar from the forest ravages it,
>> and all that move in the field feed on it.

Noted psychologist Erik Erikson believed that one of our earliest experiences of the sacred occurs when we are infants. We experience what God is like through the loving face of our mother (or our primary caregiver). It is a face of love and tenderness, and we experience being loved without condition.

Julian of Norwich, fourteenth-century English mystic, speaks of Jesus' motherly love for us: "So Jesus is our true

Mother . . . by grace. . . . He wants us to know it, for he wants to have all our love fastened on him."[3]

Imagine God's face turned toward you with such shining tenderness. God's eyes are full of love for you; God smiles at you and sings to you gently. Journal about this exercise of your imagination.

DAY 5
Entry Point
Beware

READ MARK 13:24-37.

Read again Mark 13:32-37. But about that day or hour no one knows, neither the angels in heaven, nor the Son, but only the Father. Beware, keep alert; for you do not know when the time will come. It is like a man going on a journey, when he leaves home and puts his slaves in charge, each with his work, and commands the doorkeeper to be on the watch. Therefore, keep awake—for you do not know when the master of the house will come, in the evening, or at midnight, or at cockcrow, or at dawn, or else he may find you asleep when he comes suddenly. And what I say to you I say to all: Keep awake.

Jesus tells his followers not to get distracted by cataclysmic events going on around them. They are to be spiritually aware and ready to proclaim the truth in tough times.

Do you ever face tough questions about your faith? Are you ready to give a passionate and compelling answer when asked why you have the hope that you have (see 1 Pet. 3:15)? What can you do to prepare for such a time, even though you may not know specifically what will be asked of you? How can you be ready to let the Holy Spirit speak through you?

Write your breath prayer in the journaling space. (Guidance for developing a breath prayer is found on pages 104–105 of the Leader's Guide.) Begin or end your daily devotional time by praying this prayer.

JOHN THE BAPTIST

Certain Bible characters especially capture our imagination: Noah on a boat with smelly animals for forty days and nights, Lot's wife turned to a pillar of salt, and John the Baptist, this prophet by the River Jordan wearing "clothing of camel's hair with a leather belt around his waist, and his food was locusts and wild honey" (Matt. 3:4). People went to hear him throw curses at the religious and political leaders for their sins. John the Baptist knew how to draw a crowd; he was an odd-looking character with a powerful message and the promise of salvation through repentance.

But John the Baptist was also a study in humility. Christians understand that humility is not meekness or simple respectfulness but, in the words of Charles H. Spurgeon, that "humility is to make a right estimate of oneself." John embraced his unique calling and lived as a prophet with no apologies, always trusting that God "leads the humble in what is right" (Ps. 25:9). His life and calling pointed to "one who is more powerful than I . . . ; I am not worthy to untie the thong of his sandals" (Luke 3:16).

Our challenge is to pattern our lives of discipleship after John the Baptist, boldly proclaiming the good news and choosing paths of compassion and justice that will lead others to the Messiah for whom we wait and prepare.

DAY 1

Entry Point
**Revolutionary Simplicity

READ LUKE 3:7-18.

Read again Luke 3:15-16. As the people were filled with expectation, and all were questioning in their hearts concerning John, whether he might be the Messiah, John answered all of them by saying, "I baptize you with water; but one who is more powerful than I is coming; I am not worthy to untie the thong of his sandals. He will baptize you with the Holy Spirit and fire."

John the Baptist thunders a revolutionary message that costs him his life. He is imprisoned and killed by Herod for nothing less than the radical condemnation of those in power: "Even now the ax is lying at the root of the trees" (3:9; see also 3:19). Yet when the crowd asks, "And we, what should we do?" John suggests sharing their extra coats and food with others and living honestly.

Find some cans of food and an extra jacket to take to a homeless shelter. Hold them in your hands. What might happen within you when you take them to the shelter? What revolution might take place in your heart if you chose to make generosity your lifestyle? What might happen to your need for security and control? Commit to one simple act at a time. Mark a date on your calendar a month from now; when that date arrives, assess any change you have experienced.

DAY 2

Entry Point
Zechariah's Song

Read Luke 1:67-79.

Read again Luke 1:67-72. Then his father Zechariah was filled with the Holy Spirit and spoke this prophecy: "Blessed be the Lord God of Israel, for he has looked favorably on his people and redeemed them. He has raised up a mighty savior for us in the house of his servant David, as he spoke through the mouth of his holy prophets from of old, that we would be saved from our enemies and from the hand of all who hate us. Thus he has shown the mercy promised to our ancestors, and has remembered his holy covenant."

Although many of our prayers tend to become wish lists, Zechariah's prayer acknowledges what God has done in the past and will do in the future. He worships God using the special name "Most High" and proclaims God's "tender mercy" (1:78).

Try finishing these sentences in the journaling space:

God, I praise you because you have . . .

I look forward to the day when you will . . .

O God, I am filled with awe and wonder that you . . .

DAY 3

Entry Point
Humility before God

READ PSALM 25:1-10.

Read again Psalm 25:9-10.

> He leads the humble in what is right,
>   and teaches the humble his way.
> All the paths of the LORD are steadfast love and faithfulness,
>   for those who keep his covenant and his decrees.

The psalmist says that God "leads the humble in what is right." When we become humble, we discover that God's ways are "steadfast love and faithfulness."

In what ways may God be calling you to humility in your daily life? In what ways does your schedule demand anxious efficiency rather than humble availability to God in every moment? How are you treating others you meet in your busy day?

DAY 4

Entry Point
A Day to Look Forward To

READ 2 PETER 3:8-15A.

Read again 2 Peter 3:11-15a. Since all these things are to be dissolved in this way, what sort of persons ought you to be in leading lives of holiness and godliness, waiting for and hastening the coming of the day of God, because of which the heavens will be set ablaze and dissolved, and the elements will melt with fire? But, in accordance with his promise, we wait for new heavens and a new earth, where righteousness is at home. Therefore, beloved, while you are waiting for these things, strive to be found by him at peace, without spot or blemish; and regard the patience of our Lord as salvation.

As children, most of us felt as though Christmas Day would never come. We looked forward to it eagerly for weeks—weeks that seemed like years! The anticipation filled us with excitement and imagination and prompted all kinds of preparation for the big day. Another big day is coming. But this time we don't know the date!

Suppose you knew that Jesus would return this year or next month or next week. What difference would that make in your plans and priorities? How would you feel? What preparation would you make? "Well, get on with it!" says Peter in effect. This could be the day. Let eager anticipation motivate your choices.

DAY 5

Entry Point
Good News of Comfort

READ ISAIAH 40:1-11.

Read again Isaiah 40:1-11. Comfort, O comfort my people, says your God. Speak tenderly to Jerusalem, and cry to her that she has served her term, that her penalty is paid, that she has received from the Lord's hand double for all her sins.

A voice cries out: "In the wilderness prepare the way of the LORD, make straight in the desert a highway for our God. Every valley shall be lifted up, and every mountain and hill be made low; the uneven ground shall become level, and the rough places a plain. Then the glory of the LORD shall be revealed, and all people shall see it together, for the mouth of the LORD has spoken."

A voice says, "Cry out!" And I said, "What shall I cry?" All people are grass, their constancy is like the flower of the field. The grass withers, the flower fades, when the breath of the LORD blows upon it; surely the people are grass. The grass withers, the flower fades; but the word of our God will stand forever.

Get you up to a high mountain, O Zion, herald of good tidings; lift up your voice with strength, O Jerusalem, herald of good tidings, lift it up, do not fear; say to the cities of Judah, "Here is your God!" See, the Lord GOD comes with might, and his arm rules for him; his reward is with him, and his recompense before him. He will feed his flock like a shepherd; he will gather the lambs in his arms, and carry them in his bosom, and gently lead the mother sheep.

Slowly read this famous and familiar passage, which was so important to the writers of the New Testament. Open your heart and mind to the words or phrases that seem to leap off the page at you. Write those words or phrases in the space provided here. Now pay attention to the emotions named in the text or that the text evokes in you. Ponder this cluster of words and feelings, seeing if you can discern a pattern or theme in your response to the passage. What might the Spirit be trying to show you through the patterns in your response to the Word?

Write your breath prayer here. Begin or end your daily devotional time by praying it.

WEEK
THREE

MARY

Theotokos is the Greek title that Eastern Orthodox and Eastern Catholic churches use for Mary the mother of Jesus. Its English translation is "God-bearer"—a beautiful image of Mary, literally and figuratively, bearing Jesus to the world. We could pity Mary as an unwed pregnant teenager. We could worship her obedience and enshrine her in paintings and icons. We could marginalize her as inconsequential to the big story of Jesus' life, death, and resurrection.

Or we can learn from Mary. Frightened and perplexed by the angel's announcement, young Mary quickly regains her composure to ask a clarifying question; she then accepts her role in God's plan with trust and obedience: "Here am I, the servant of the Lord; let it be with me according to your word" (Luke 1:38). Mary's life has been upended, her engagement threatened, her reputation ruined, her future forever altered. Yet at every turn, Mary takes time to ponder her circumstances and treasure each new wrinkle as a blessing. She exemplifies the guidance of the Old Testament prophets—casting out fear, like Zephaniah, and singing praises to God, like Isaiah.

This Advent we will not only meet the Messiah again but also have the chance to be God-bearers: to introduce friends, family, and strangers to the love of God come to earth.

DAY 1

Entry Point
Treasuring . . .

READ LUKE 2:41-52.

Read again Luke 2:41-52. Now every year his parents went to Jerusalem for the festival of the Passover. And when he was twelve years old, they went up as usual for the festival. When the festival was ended and they started to return, the boy Jesus stayed behind in Jerusalem, but his parents did not know it. Assuming that he was in the group of travelers, they went a day's journey. Then they started to look for him among their relatives and friends. When they did not find him, they returned to Jerusalem to search for him. After three days they found him in the temple, sitting among the teachers, listening to them and asking them questions. And all who heard him were amazed at his understanding and his answers. When his parents saw him they were astonished; and his mother said to him, "Child, why have you treated us like this? Look, your father and I have been searching for you in great anxiety." He said to them, "Why were you searching for me? Did you not know that I must be in my Father's house?" But they did not understand what he said to them. Then he went down with them and came to Nazareth, and was obedient to them. His mother treasured all these things in her heart. And Jesus increased in wisdom and in years, and in divine and human favor.

Mary reacts to crises by pondering or treasuring in her heart what God says or does. She does this when she faces the shame of becoming an unwed mother; when she responds to the shepherds' visit in a stable; and, in this passage, when she copes with the increasing independence of her twelve-year-old son (1:29; 2:19, 51).

Consider how Mary's response might be an example to you. How could you respond more contemplatively and prayerfully to circumstances or happenings in your life? What situation or event calls for pondering instead of worrying, fixing, or withdrawing?

DAY 2

Entry Point
From Disaster to Celebration

Read Zephaniah 3:14-20.

Read again Zephaniah 3:14-20. Sing aloud, O daughter Zion; shout, O Israel! Rejoice and exult with all your heart, O daughter Jerusalem! The Lord has taken away the judgments against you, he has turned away your enemies. The king of Israel, the Lord, is in your midst; you shall fear disaster no more. On that day it shall be said to Jerusalem: Do not fear, O Zion; do not let your hands grow weak. The Lord, your God, is in your midst, a warrior who gives victory; he will rejoice over you with gladness, he will renew you in his love; he will exult over you with loud singing as on a day of festival. I will remove disaster from you, so that you will not bear reproach for it. I will deal with all your oppressors at that time. And I will save the lame and gather the outcast, and I will change their shame into praise and renown in all the earth. At that time I will bring you home, at the time when I gather you; for I will make you renowned and praised among all the peoples of the earth, when I restore your fortunes before your eyes, says the Lord.

In the middle of troubles and pain, there is a promise of joy. The threat of destruction is over, and hope springs up once again. In the same way a mother might comfort a child she has disciplined, God reminds his people of his great love.

Reread the passage slowly, noting words or phrases of promise that particularly speak to you.

Use these words or phrases to write a prayer based on this passage. Ask God to fulfill the promises you are waiting on to be fulfilled. Praise God for making such wonderful promises.

DAY 3

Entry Point
**Opening Your Heart to God

Read Isaiah 12:2-6.

Read again Isaiah 12:2-6. Surely God is my salvation; I will trust, and will not be afraid, for the Lord God is my strength and my might; he has become my salvation. With joy you will draw water from the wells of salvation.

And you will say in that day: Give thanks to the Lord, call on his name; make known his deeds among the nations; proclaim that his name is exalted. Sing praises to the Lord, for he has done gloriously; let this be known in all the earth. Shout aloud and sing for joy, O royal Zion, for great in your midst is the Holy One of Israel.

This exultant passage is traditionally used in Jewish prayer as part of the *havdalah*, a ceremony that marks the end of the sabbath, because it looks ahead to the final redemption God promises to Israel and the nations. It is easy to give thanks and sing praise to God when life is going well and our blessings overflow. We find it more difficult to offer the same songs of praise in the midst of trials, doubts, and hardships.

Whether your cup overflows with the hope and joy of the season or you find yourself overwhelmed by fear and trouble, recite this song of praise or chant it in a monotone or to a simple melody.

Continue to recite the song, opening your heart and mind to God's goodness. Journal here about your response to this exercise.

DAY 4

Entry Point
Inventory of Peace

READ PHILIPPIANS 4:4-7.

Read again Philippians 4:4-7. Rejoice in the Lord always; again I will say, Rejoice. Let your gentleness be known to everyone. The Lord is near. Do not worry about anything, but in everything by prayer and supplication with thanksgiving let your requests be made known to God. And the peace of God, which surpasses all understanding, will guard your hearts and your minds in Christ Jesus.

What images and impressions does the word *peace* create for you? The word *peace* has rich biblical connotations of reconciliation, wholeness, health, and unity. The apostle Paul often greets fellow Christians with the words *grace* and *peace* (see Rom. 1:7; 1 Cor. 1:3; Gal. 1:3).

Read and ponder these words of scripture. Look at the two column headings on the opposite page. In the left column list some of the things that rob you of peace. In the right column note what gives you a sense of peace. Which column reflects the condition you find yourself in most often? How might this scripture passage guide you into greater peace?

What robs me of peace?	What gives me peace?

DAY 5

Entry Point
Advice

READ 1 THESSALONIANS 5:16-24.

Read again 1 Thessalonians 5:16-18. Rejoice always, pray without ceasing, give thanks in all circumstances; for this is the will of God in Christ Jesus for you.

In the First Letter to the Thessalonians, we get to eavesdrop on a personal and endearing letter from Paul to a community that reveals his affection, his pride in them, and his desire to be their religious instructor. As he wraps up the letter in these final verses, Paul gives clear and concise advice for discipleship: rejoice always, pray without ceasing, give thanks in all circumstances.

Paul's advice holds as true for the Thessalonians as this attitude did for Mary, the God-bearer. Which piece of advice do you most need to hear right now? Write the advice on a small slip of paper or sticky note and keep it visible today as a reminder of God's desire for you to be kept sound in spirit and soul and body. Later, take time to record your response to this experiment on these pages.

Write your breath prayer, and begin or end your daily devotional time by praying it.

THE SHEPHERDS

The good news of Jesus' birth comes first to the shepherds, humble and hardworking people, tending to their flock by night. God knew these men could not bring gifts of gold, frankincense, and myrrh, as the wise men who would arrive later. Immanuel, "God with us," came among us in a manger where all could come and kneel to worship him. There were no barriers of dress code, entrance fees, or guards at the door. From his first breath, God was available to all.

In the revelation to the shepherds, God has revealed God's heart and character: "the angel choir breaking into the darkness of earth's night to herald the long-awaited sunrise, assuring the humble poor that whatever the mighty governments of the world might be doing, God cares for people, and with a shepherd's heart."[4]

Each of the readings this week reveals the "shepherd's heart," humility and awe before the created world and the mystery of God. Jesus is born in the city of Bethlehem, "one of the little clans of Judah" (Mic. 5:2). And the praise of God echoes in the heavens and the seas from the fields and the trees (Ps. 96).

DAY 1

Entry Point
Singing with Angels

READ LUKE 2:8-20.

Read again Luke 2:13-18. And suddenly there was with the angel a multitude of the heavenly host, praising God and saying, "Glory to God in the highest heaven, and on earth peace among those whom he favors!" When the angels had left them and gone into heaven, the shepherds said to one another, "Let us go now to Bethlehem and see this thing that has taken place, which the Lord has made known to us." So they went with haste and found Mary and Joseph, and the child lying in the manger. When they saw this, they made known what had been told them about this child; and all who heard it were amazed at what the shepherds told them.

Everyone is singing—Mary (1:46–55), Zechariah, Simeon (2:28–32), the angels! Sing a song of praise—such as "Angels We Have Heard on High" (especially the chorus)—in the shower, in the woods, or in the car. Sing where no one can hear you so that you can sing exuberantly and can embellish your song of praise with worshipful gestures or movements. Experiment with the joy of worshiping God— let inward singing permeate your activities. Another option: Sing the African-American spiritual "Guide My Feet" (based on Luke 1:79).

Journal about your singing and praising experience.

DAY 2

Entry Point
The One of Peace

READ MICAH 5:2-5A.

Read again Micah 5:2-5a. But you, O Bethlehem of Ephra-thah, who are one of the little clans of Judah, from you shall come forth for me one who is to rule in Israel, whose origin is from of old, from ancient days. Therefore he shall give them up until the time when she who is in labor has brought forth; then the rest of his kindred shall return to the people of Israel. And he shall stand and feed his flock in the strength of the LORD, in the majesty of the name of the LORD his God. And they shall live secure, for now he shall be great to the ends of the earth; and he shall be the one of peace.

In this passage Micah describes a future deliverer who will once and for all time restore Judah to its rightful place among the nations. The source of this new leader's power is proclaimed in verses 4-5. If asked to describe a powerful and influential leader, most would not choose the image of a shepherd, but we hear Jesus and the coming kingdom compared again and again to shepherds throughout the scriptures.

What do you hear in these verses, and in the life of a shepherd, about leadership? Consider the areas in your life where you serve in a leadership role—perhaps on your block, at work, among friends, with children. Reflect on your leadership in the light of these verses and note your thoughts.

DAY 3
Entry Point
**The Call to Unending Worship

READ PSALM 96.

Read again Psalm 96:8–13.

> Ascribe to the LORD the glory due his name;
>> bring an offering, and come into his courts.
> Worship the LORD in holy splendor;
>> tremble before him, all the earth.
>
> Say among the nations, "The LORD is king!
>> The world is firmly established; it shall never be moved.
>> He will judge the peoples with equity."
> Let the heavens be glad, and let the earth rejoice;
>> let the sea roar, and all that fills it;
> let the field exult, and everything in it.
> Then shall all the trees of the forest sing for joy
>> before the LORD; for he is coming,
>> for he is coming to judge the earth.
> He will judge the world with righteousness,
>> and the peoples with his truth.

As the shepherds stood in the field that night, they may have recalled these words from the psalm, for surely the heavens were glad and the field exulting in praise of the coming of the Lord. Their spirits joined the angels singing in heaven celebrating love's fulfillment. Jan van Ruysbroek (1294–1381), a Flemish mystic and priest, described worship this way:

This flowing of God demands evermore a flowing back again; for God is a sea, ebbing and flowing, ceaselessly flowing into each one of His elect. . . . And therefore all spirits evermore are gathered together and form one burning flame in love, so that they may bring to perfection the work of loving God according to [God's] excellence. To the reason it is plain that this work is impossible for God's creatures. But love will always perfect love.[5]

How can you join the shepherds' song this Advent? Take time today to celebrate the Lord's birth in the glory of nature and note your reflections.

DAY 4

Entry Point
To God Be the Glory

READ ROMANS 16:25-27.

Read again Romans 16:25–27. Now to God who is able to strengthen you according to my gospel and the proclamation of Jesus Christ, according to the revelation of the mystery that was kept secret for long ages but is now disclosed, and through the prophetic writings is made known to all the Gentiles, according to the command of the eternal God, to bring about the obedience of faith—to the only wise God, through Jesus Christ, to whom be the glory forever! Amen.

God has made known to us the mystery of faith: we can know God in an intimate way through the incarnation of Jesus Christ. God is accessible and available. God is "for us," and that is reason to shout and to sing: "To the only wise God, through Jesus Christ, to whom be the glory forever! Amen."

Let these last verses become a dialogue with God as you pray them. What particular word or phrase draws your attention? As you keep that word or phrase in your mind, let God lead you further: what do you need to disclose? How do you need to be strengthened? comforted? What prompts you to cry, "Glory to God"? Return to these verses again, changing the wording so that it becomes your personal response to who God is and what God has done.

DAY 5

Entry Point
A Question to Ponder

READ ACTS 1:6-11.

Read again Acts 1:6–11. So when they had come together, they asked him, "Lord, is this the time when you will restore the kingdom to Israel?" He replied, "It is not for you to know the times or periods that the Father has set by his own authority. But you will receive power when the Holy Spirit has come upon you; and you will be my witnesses in Jerusalem, in all Judea and Samaria, and to the ends of the earth." When he had said this, as they were watching, he was lifted up, and a cloud took him out of their sight. While he was going and they were gazing up toward heaven, suddenly two men in white robes stood by them. They said, "Men of Galilee, why do you stand looking up toward heaven? This Jesus, who has been taken up from you into heaven, will come in the same way as you saw him go into heaven."

Here we again find men, like the shepherds in Luke, looking up toward heaven. How were these two events similar? How were they different?

Do you sometimes allow prayer, Bible study, or other spiritual exercises to become substitutes for your mission as a Christian rather than the power sources for that mission?

Write a dialogue between you and God. Begin with God asking you what the angels asked, "Why do you stand looking up toward heaven?" How would you respond? What do you think God would say to your response? Writing it out will keep the dialogue focused.

Write your breath prayer here, and begin or end your daily devotional time by praying it.

JESUS

It's good that you are continuing your devotions now that Christmas Day has passed. The child is born, the songs are sung, the stockings have been hung, and the trash has been put out at the curb, but Christmas is actually just beginning!

The season of Advent, of our expectant waiting, has finished and now we move into the season of Christmastide. Christmas, literally *Christ Mass*, is the feast of the Incarnation, the celebration of God becoming human in the person of Jesus. Outside of the Catholic and Orthodox churches and a few others, the idea of Christmas as a season has nearly disappeared. But the Christmas season in most Western church traditions begins at sunset on Christmas Eve, December 24, and lasts through January 5. This twelve-day period is known in many places as the Twelve Days of Christmas.

You can see these remaining days of Christmastide as a gift. With the celebration and busyness of the holiday behind you, take advantage of this coming week to consider the reality of Jesus' presence in your life, in your family, and in the world. Jesus' arrival in the world is marked by light, peace, joy, and justice. Where do you long for these gifts in your life? Where is the world in need? How can you invite Christ or bear Christ into the dark and despairing places as you continue to celebrate Christmas?

DAY 1

Entry Point
A Light Shines

READ JOHN 1:1-14.

Read again John 1:1-14. In the beginning was the Word, and the Word was with God, and the Word was God. He was in the beginning with God. All things came into being through him, and without him not one thing came into being. What has come into being in him was life, and the life was the light of all people.

The light shines in the darkness, and the darkness did not overcome it. There was a man sent from God, whose name was John. He came as a witness to testify to the light, so that all might believe through him. He himself was not the light, but he came to testify to the light. The true light, which enlightens everyone, was coming into the world. He was in the world, and the world came into being through him; yet the world did not know him. He came to what was his own, and his own people did not accept him. But to all who received him, who believed in his name, he gave power to become children of God, who were born, not of blood or of the will of the flesh or of the will of man, but of God. And the Word became flesh and lived among us, and we have seen his glory, the glory as of a father's only son, full of grace and truth.

John's rich, resonating words ring out like a majestic overture. Imagine trumpets and drums as the great themes of this gospel are declared: "In the beginning was the Word"; "in him was life"; "the light shines"; "darkness did not overcome it." Walk around the room, reading this passage again aloud, as loudly as the text suggests to you. As you read, listen for a word or phrase that catches your attention. Repeat it and let it expand within your spirit. Sense its power. Give it center stage in your consciousness, and let it speak to you.

When you are ready, use this experience as the foundation for a prayer of reflection.

DAY 2

Entry Point
God with Us

READ ISAIAH 7:10-16.

Read again Isaiah 7:14. Therefore the Lord himself will give you a sign. Look, the young woman is with child and shall bear a son, and shall name him Immanuel.

The sign of "Immanuel" is intended to give Ahaz and the people courage in spite of their shaking hearts (7:2). What makes your heart shake? Prayerfully imagine a situation or person that has brought you fear. Now let some tangible sign of Immanuel—God with you—become part of the scene. It may be the light of the Spirit in or around you, the presence of Jesus beside you, or an affirmative phrase on your lips. Let the sense of that presence strengthen you as you continue to face what you fear. Consider imaginatively how you might act differently in the face of your fear, claiming God's abiding presence.

DAY 3

Entry Point
Joy throughout the Earth

READ PSALM 98.

Read again Psalm 98:4–9.

Make a joyful noise to the LORD, all the earth;
   break forth into joyous song and sing praises.
Sing praises to the LORD with the lyre,
   with the lyre and the sound of melody.
With trumpets and the sound of the horn
   make a joyful noise before the King, the LORD.
Let the sea roar, and all that fills it;
   the world and those who live in it.
Let the floods clap their hands;
   let the hills sing together for joy
at the presence of the LORD, for he is coming
   to judge the earth.
He will judge the world with righteousness,
   and the peoples with equity.

Praise is not limited to human creatures. While the psalmist utters praise with his mouth, the earth raises a "joyful noise" in countless ways. God enjoys the brilliant color of a wildflower in the middle of a deserted field, a young lion running in tall grass, and an ocean with its panoply of life. Our praise is not isolated from the rest of creation's.

Make an appointment with nature to sit in awe or take a walk, joining your thanks to the praise of God throughout the earth.

DAY 4

Entry Point
The Royal Child

READ ISAIAH 9:1-7.

Read again Isaiah 9:1-7. But there will be no gloom for those who were in anguish. In the former time he brought into contempt the land of Zebulun and the land of Naphtali, but in the latter time he will make glorious the way of the sea, the land beyond the Jordan, Galilee of the nations. The people who walked in darkness have seen a great light; those who lived in a land of deep darkness— on them light has shined. You have multiplied the nation, you have increased its joy; they rejoice before you as with joy at the harvest, as people exult when dividing plunder. For the yoke of their burden, and the bar across their shoulders, the rod of their oppressor, you have broken as on the day of Midian. For all the boots of the tramping warriors and all the garments rolled in blood shall be burned as fuel for the fire. For a child has been born for us, a son given to us; authority rests upon his shoulders; and he is named Wonderful Counselor, Mighty God, Everlasting Father, Prince of Peace. His authority shall grow continually, and there shall be endless peace for the throne of David and his kingdom. He will establish and uphold it with justice and with righteousness from this time onward and forevermore. The zeal of the LORD of hosts will do this.

Take time to enter deeply into this vision about the coming of the royal child by reading the passage aloud to yourself and then prayerfully allowing your imagination to give life to the sequence of images in the text.

Envision the light dawning on people who live in great darkness; the breaking of the bar of oppression; the stilling of the fever of war; the appearance of the divinely given child who brings the time of justice and peace. Let yourself see the child vividly; perhaps the child is shining with God's light. Imagine that light touching your life. Imagine the light bringing light to the darkness in the world. You might accompany your meditation with selections from Handel's *Messiah* if you have a recording, or use favorite Christmas hymns or anthems.

DAY 5

Entry Point
**The Reflection of God's Glory

READ HEBREWS 1:1-4.

Read again Hebrews 1:1-4. Long ago God spoke to our ancestors in many and various ways by the prophets, but in these last days he has spoken to us by a Son, whom he appointed heir of all things, through whom he also created the worlds. He is the reflection of God's glory and the exact imprint of God's very being, and he sustains all things by his powerful word. When he had made purification for sins, he sat down at the right hand of the Majesty on high, having become as much superior to angels as the name he has inherited is more excellent than theirs.

Jesus Christ is the Son of God! Consider what that means to God. Then consider what that means to you. Notice what God has done through Jesus (spoken, created, sustained, and saved). List some of the ways you have experienced this "superior" ministry of Jesus Christ in your life.

After reading and pondering this passage, close your eyes and imagine how you would depict Jesus through painting, sculpture, music, or poetry based on this scripture. What characteristics of Jesus would you try to emphasize? You might want to create the work of art you have imagined.

Write your breath prayer here, and begin or end your daily devotional time by praying it.

THE MAGI

This week we journey to Epiphany with the Magi. The word *epiphany* means "appearance" or "manifestation." Popular usage likens *epiphany* to words such as *eureka* or *aha!* For some English speakers it conjures images of a light bulb coming on, or of seeing something once hidden from view. Epiphany invites believers to consider the many ways that people came to understand who Jesus was and is for us today.

The wise men, or Magi, who brought gifts to the child Jesus were the first Gentiles to acknowledge Jesus as "King," and so were the first to "show" or "reveal" Jesus to a wider world as the incarnate Christ. This act of worship by the Magi, which corresponded to Simeon's blessing Jesus as the future "light for revelation to the Gentiles" (Luke 2:32), indicated that Jesus came for all people of all nations, of all races, and that God's work in the world would not be limited to a few.

The wise men's journey took them outside their country and their comfort zone. The Magi risked the consequences of disobeying Herod, known to behave like a madman when provoked, and they returned home by another way. Consider your journey of discipleship. Where has it taken you beyond your comfort zone? Who have you traveled with? Where does that path lead from here? Be open to aha! moments as you journey with the wise men this week.

DAY 1

Entry Point
Reasons of the Heart

READ MATTHEW 2:1-12.

Read again Matthew 2:2. Where is the child who has been born king of the Jews? For we observed his star at its rising, and have come to pay him homage.

The Magi come to worship Jesus. Later, others come to Jesus for healing and forgiveness, to learn from him, or in hopes of gaining material blessings or power.

Imagine you are a contemporary of Jesus, and you have just heard about him. Who told you about Jesus? What did that person say about Jesus? What was the first thing you said? What did you think about just before falling asleep that night? What do you seek now? Ask God to help you find it. Or ask God to teach you, as you read this Gospel, what you should be seeking.

DAY 2

Entry Point
Pilgrimage

READ PSALM 122.

Read again Psalm 122.

> I was glad when they said to me,
>> "Let us go to the house of the LORD!"
> Our feet are standing
>> within your gates, O Jerusalem.
>
> Jerusalem—built as a city
>> that is bound firmly together.
> To it the tribes go up,
>> the tribes of the LORD,
> as was decreed for Israel,
>> to give thanks to the name of the LORD.
> For there the thrones for judgment were set up,
>> the thrones of the house of David.
>
> Pray for the peace of Jerusalem:
>> "May they prosper who love you.
> Peace be within your walls,
>> and security within your towers."
> For the sake of my relatives and friends
>> I will say, "Peace be within you."
> For the sake of the house of the LORD our God,
>> I will seek your good.

We hear about people going on pilgrimages more frequently these days—to Israel, to Ireland, to Scotland—much like the wise men, who made pilgrimage to pay homage to the Christ child. A pilgrimage can take you to an old family home or the church of your childhood or to a place of particular Christian significance for your faith journey. Even if you cannot travel physically, you may do so in spirit. Using colored pencils, markers, or paints, draw a picture of a "sacred place." Below your picture, write a word that comes to mind as you recall or imagine this place.

DAY 3

Entry Point
Setting Our Sights on Jesus

READ JOHN 10:14-17.

Read again John 10:14–17. I am the good shepherd. I know my own and my own know me, just as the Father knows me and I know the Father. And I lay down my life for the sheep. I have other sheep that do not belong to this fold. I must bring them also, and they will listen to my voice. So there will be one flock, one shepherd. For this reason the Father loves me, because I lay down my life in order to take it up again.

The Magi set out to find Jesus by way of unknown land-scapes, guided by a star and by the directions of King Herod. They were willing to face barriers of all kinds to find and worship Jesus.

What lies ahead of you right now? With crayon or paint, draw or paint a picture of it. Are you walking into green pastures or dark valleys? Incorporate Jesus in your picture. Think about the implications of Jesus' presence. Envisioning Jesus ahead of you as you walk, pray about what is happening to you.

DAY 4

Entry Point
**Don't Forget

Read Deuteronomy 8:1-20.

Read again Deuteronomy 8:7-16. For the Lord your God is bringing you into a good land, a land with flowing streams, with springs and underground waters welling up in valleys and hills, a land of wheat and barley, of vines and fig trees and pomegranates, a land of olive trees and honey, a land where you may eat bread without scarcity, where you will lack nothing, a land whose stones are iron and from whose hills you may mine copper. You shall eat your fill and bless the Lord your God for the good land that he has given you.

Take care that you do not forget the Lord your God, by failing to keep his commandments, his ordinances, and his statutes, which I am commanding you today. When you have eaten your fill and have built fine houses and live in them, and when your herds and flocks have multiplied, and your silver and gold is multiplied, and all that you have is multiplied, then do not exalt yourself, forgetting the Lord your God, who brought you out of the land of Egypt, out of the house of slavery, who led you through the great and terrible wilderness, an arid wasteland with poisonous snakes and scorpions. He made water flow for you from flint rock, and fed you in the wilderness with manna that your ancestors did not know, to humble you and to test you, and in the end to do you good.

Moses declares that God is eager to bless the Israelites. Go through chapter 8 and write down the types of blessings Moses promises in the future (particularly vv. 7-10, 12-13). Next, compare the future blessings with the past sojourn in the desert (particularly vv. 4, 14-16).

Consider your life before and after you began actively following God. Have any blessings tempted you to forget your need for God? Have you forgotten what life was like without God? How can your memory of God's deliverance in the past enhance your thankfulness today? How can you fully enjoy God's blessings without losing sight of the One who provided them?

DAY 5

Entry Point
God's Work Will Be Completed

Read Philippians 1:3-11.

Read again Philippians 1:3-11. I thank my God every time I remember you, constantly praying with joy in every one of my prayers for all of you, because of your sharing in the gospel from the first day until now. I am confident of this, that the one who began a good work among you will bring it to completion by the day of Jesus Christ.

It is right for me to think this way about all of you, because you hold me in your heart, for all of you share in God's grace with me, both in my imprisonment and in the defense and confirmation of the gospel. For God is my witness, how I long for all of you with the compassion of Christ Jesus.

And this is my prayer, that your love may overflow more and more with knowledge and full insight to help you to determine what is best, so that in the day of Christ you may be pure and blameless, having produced the harvest of righteousness that comes through Jesus Christ for the glory and praise of God.

Paul warmly and joyfully expresses confidence that God will complete the work of faith and growth in those who are in Christ Jesus. Paul's prayer is that his readers may grow in love, discernment, and the fruit of righteousness.

It's important to look at where we've been and where God is taking us in our spiritual lives (see Pss. 77:11; 105:5; 143:5). If you have been following Jesus for a number of years, recall what your life was like at the beginning of your journey. How have you grown? If you have become a Christian recently, reflect on the promises and faithfulness of God, who calls you to spiritual maturity. What specific aspect of hope or encouragement does this passage offer?

Write your breath prayer here, and begin or end your daily devotional time by praying it.

LEADER'S GUIDE

Meeting the Messiah does not assume that the persons in your group have never met the Messiah. The seasons of Advent, Christmas, and Epiphany present an opportunity to meet the Messiah *again*. The mystery and power of the Holy Scriptures is that they are alive, offering wisdom, inspiration, and guidance each time they are read with an open mind and willing spirit. During this Advent and Christmastide, disciples are invited to read the scriptures not as a backdrop to the shopping and baking and parties but as *the* story and *the* focus of all their actions.

The Holy Spirit introduces us to Jesus each year, just as the Spirit gave visions to the prophets, called Mary, guided John the Baptist, appeared to the shepherds, became incarnate in Jesus, and traveled with the Magi. Each week participants in this study will be invited to reconsider the different ways and circumstances of those who first met the Messiah and to prepare for their own meeting with Jesus in the coming season.

OVERVIEW OF *MEETING THE MESSIAH*

You will be leading an exploration of scripture about meeting the Messiah over a period of six weeks—the four weeks of Advent plus two weeks following Christmas leading to Epiphany. The study builds on daily Bible readings (five per week) and personal exploration exercises (entry points) tied to the daily readings. The theme of the study is a reintroduction to the Messiah through the perspectives of the Holy Spirit, John the Baptist, Mary, the shepherds, Jesus himself, and the Magi. You and your group will be engaged in an interactive reading of familiar Bible stories. Using the senses and the imagination, you will prepare to meet the Messiah amidst the hustle and bustle of cultural celebrations of the holiday season.

TIME COMMITMENT

The daily Bible readings and responses require ten to fifteen minutes a day. These lead up to and become the starting point for weekly small-group meetings. This leader's guide includes a process and resources for six weekly meetings. You may choose either a 45-minute or a 90-minute format for these gatherings. Your first session needs to be at least 60 minutes to allow for community-building activities and a general introduction to *Meeting the Messiah*. Be sure participants have their books ahead of time. They need to read the introductory material and Week 1 before your first gathering.

Meetings in the 90-minute format will include a practice called *lectio divina* (listening to God in scripture) in each session; the 45-minute format does not include group *lectio* each week. This accounts for the time difference between the two formats. Detailed directions for leading *lectio divina* follow this introduction.

GROUP SIZE

Each element of the sessions has a suggested time frame for a group size of nine. A larger group will be unable to complete the activities in the suggested time. If you attempt to discuss in the whole group rather than in smaller groups of three, time will not allow completion of the activities. Therefore, try to limit each group to no more than nine persons and to discuss in groups of three. For a larger group, you will need to reduce the time spent on each element or omit a portion from the session plan.

INTRODUCING THE STUDY AT THE FIRST SESSION

At the group's first meeting, you will present the approach, process, and content of the study as a whole. *Meeting the Messiah* is based on formational scripture reading, which may seem a dramatic departure from the analytical methods that often characterize Bible study. The first meeting provides a chance for participants to become acquainted with the difference between *formational* and *informational* reading of the Bible. The chart on page 16 summarizes those differences. This background will allow participants to get the most from their daily readings from the outset.

PREPARING THE MEETING SPACE

The activities in this study aim to engage participants on sensory and emotional, or affective, levels. A welcoming and worshipful atmosphere will foster those experiences. You may set up a worship center on a small table, using seasonal decorations that change weekly. Or you may develop a worship center with an Advent wreath, a Christ candle, a cross, or other symbols. A group member may have special gifts for creating such worship arrangements. Before or during the first session, ask for volunteers who would prepare the worship center weekly.

Music can add depth to the sessions. If you cannot lead singing, ask for a volunteer from the group to help with music/singing during opening and closing worship and prayer times. Compile a list of appropriate songs from songbooks and hymnals available in your meeting place, and give these to the music leader before the first session. You may want to use the same hymn, chorus, or song to begin and end a session, so that you need to choose only six.

Each session will include conversation in groups of three about the week's readings and entry-point responses, so a setting where you can easily rearrange chairs from a large circle to triads is ideal.

When sessions include handouts, place these on chairs or tables before participants arrive. Having them in place reduces confusion and creates a more peaceful atmosphere.

LOOKING AHEAD: PREPARING FOR THE SESSIONS

Always have newsprint or a whiteboard and markers, extra Bibles, paper and writing utensils, name tags. Use this checklist for preparation:

- Do the daily readings and entry-point activities for the week. Assemble materials required for the session.

- Review the Exploring the Word activity until you feel ready to lead it.

- Review instructions for leading *lectio divina* and photocopy and/or mark the week's passage for the alternate reader.

- Prepare materials for worship center (or remind the volunteer).

- Choose an appropriate song to sing at opening and closing of session (or remind the volunteer to prepare).

LEADING *LECTIO DIVINA* IN GROUPS
(for 90-minute sessions)

Lectio divina is a Latin phrase often translated as "spiritual reading" or "holy reading." But for the first fifteen hundred years of the Christian church, people learned and absorbed the words and stories of scripture by *hearing* them read. Scrolls and books were rare, and most people could not read. Personal copies of the Bible in the language of ordinary life were not available until long after the invention of the printing press in the mid-1400s, and even then only to the wealthy. So when we hear scripture being read, we sit in company with the first saints who listened to hear God's personal word to them through the words of the Bible.

If you have never led *lectio divina*, the process outlined here may seem too simple to be effective. Please trust the approach. In a few sessions you will see God at work as participants grow in their eagerness and ability to hear God speak to them through the words of scripture. The group reflection on scripture is an invaluable part of this study. The time investment is worth the return for the participants.

Lectio divina is based on hearing a passage of scripture read several times. Using the instructions below, you will guide group members in listening, reflecting in silence, talking with others, and praying in response to what they have heard. Allowing silence may be the most difficult part of the process for both leader and participants. Don't rush the silence; use a watch with a second hand to be sure you allow ample time for each step.

PREPARING THE GROUP TO LISTEN

Before the first session of *lectio divina*, reflect together on "Obstacles to Hearing God in Scripture" (page 17). Ask group members to think about all the things we do instead of listening—analyzing, classifying, and so on. The first two steps in the *lectio* process may be the most demanding because they require listening and silence. In the first step, you will invite group members to listen for a word or phrase from the Bible passage you read and to consider it in silence. The second tough step comes when you direct them to repeat only that word or phrase within their small group. They speak it aloud without comment or elaboration.

We are so accustomed to analyzing, to stepping back from scripture to think about what it means, that we often do not listen to the words themselves. For instance, if we read aloud the story of the persistent widow from Luke 18:1-8, some people will think and say within their group the word *perseverance,* but that word does not appear in the passage. That word and others like it (*compassion, mercy, faith*) are thoughts about the passage that reflect our analysis rather than words we actually heard. Try to help group members realize that they are to listen for a *word* or *phrase* that occurs in the passage, *not* come up with a word to describe the passage. The goal is not to analyze or categorize the reading.

Before you begin, invite group members to sit in groups of three, to get comfortable, and to prepare for a time of listening to scripture. Explain that they will be hearing a passage of scripture—the same passage—read several times and that each reading will be followed by silence for reflection. Ask them to trust you to guide them through the process. Suggest that they give themselves fully to hearing the scripture—not reading along in their own Bibles but listening.

On the third reading, a group member will read the passage aloud so participants will hear it in a voice other than yours. Ask for a volunteer to do this before beginning. Read the passage from the same translation each time to avoid distracting people by differences between the translations. You may want to photocopy the Bible page containing each session's *lectio divina* passage and mark the reading to make the change of readers less intrusive and to be sure the same translation is used. Tell participants that the small groups will not be "reporting" to the entire body in any way; what they say within their smaller groups will remain private.

STEP-BY-STEP GUIDE TO *LECTIO DIVINA*

Use these instructions each time you lead *lectio divina* with your group in the coming weeks.

STEP ONE: (first reading) Tell the group members that you will read the passage twice, once to orient them to its overall content and again, more slowly, so that they can listen for a word or phrase that stops them or gets their attention. Read the passage aloud, twice. Then say, **In the silence, repeat your word or phrase to yourself and reflect on it.**

Allow one to two minutes of silence. Time this step so you do not rush.

STEP TWO: Say, **Within your group, repeat the word or phrase that attracted you—without comment, summary, or analysis. You may choose to pass.**

STEP THREE: (second reading) Ask group members to listen as you read the passage again, slowly, being open to how it connects to them. Tell them that their word or phrase may or may not be the same one on this reading as during the first reading. After reading, say, **In silence, consider how your word or phrase connects to your life right now—a situation, a feeling, a possibility.**

Allow three minutes of silence for reflection.

STEP FOUR: Remind the group that participants may always choose not to speak by saying "Pass" when their turn comes. Say, **In your groups, take a few minutes each to tell about the connection you sense between your life and your word or phrase. Or you may pass.**

Ask the person closest to you in each group to speak first.

STEP FIVE: (third-stage reading) Ask the alternate reader to read the passage again, slowly. Invite group members to listen during this reading for an invitation from God for the next few days. Say, **In the silence, consider what invitation you hear from God. Be open to a sensory impression, an image, a song, a fragrance.**

Allow three minutes of silence for reflection.

STEP SIX: Ask group members to ponder in silence the invitation they heard.

Allow several minutes of silence.

STEP SEVEN: Invite each person to speak about the invitation he or she senses from God for his or her life in the next few days. Say, **In your groups, allow each person to tell about the invitation he or she heard. Or you may pass.**

This time, have the person farthest from you begin. This is an important step in the process, so allow ample time for each person to speak. Watch the groups; check to see which are finishing up, which need more time. Do not rush the process.

STEP EIGHT: Invite persons to pray for each other, one by one in turn, within their smaller groups. Ask each individual to pray for the person to his or her right. The group members can decide whether they will pray aloud or silently. Say, **Pray for each other to be empowered to respond to the invitations you heard. You may pray silently or aloud.**

Remind participants to remain silent when their group finishes praying, since other groups may still be in prayer. When all have finished praying, say, **Amen.**

You may debrief this experience of *lectio divina* by asking the group for comments. Point out that everyone responds differently to the various ways of exploring scripture; there is no expected outcome. Try some of these questions to generate discussion: *What worked for you? What was difficult about responding to scripture this way? Have you been led through this process before? If so, what was different, better, or worse this time?*

Session 1

The Holy Spirit

Note: Session 1 requires at least 60 minutes to allow for getting acquainted and general introduction to the study as well as exercises related to the first week's readings; add 40 to 45 minutes if you want to include the practice of *lectio divina* (Engaging the Word). All other session plans are designed for 90 minutes. If you will use this study in 45-minute sessions, omit the *lectio divina* experience (Engaging the Word) each time.

Assemble materials: pictures for Exploring the Word; prewritten questions for the activity. Write the words *presence, prayer, preparation, participation, confidentiality*, and *courtesy* on newsprint or a board.

OPENING PRAYER (5 minutes)

Light the Christ candle, saying something like: **Each week we will light a Christ candle to welcome Christ into our conversation. It will remain lighted during the session as a reminder that we are engaged in holy conversation as we meet here. Let's pray.** Read this prayer or pray spontaneously, as you wish.

> Holy and loving God, as we enter into this season of expectant waiting, be born anew in our hearts and spirits. Be with us in these sessions as we reflect on the ancient story of Jesus' birth, revealing yourself anew. As we journey toward Christmas, show us how to bear witness to the light of Christ in the world. Amen.

COMMUNITY BUILDING (10 minutes)

Welcome everyone to the study and tell them this session will allow time to get to know one another a bit better and learn what to expect during the coming weeks of *Meeting the Messiah.*

Introductions: Have persons introduce themselves. Give people one minute to say whatever they choose about themselves, including what they are most looking forward to this Advent. (If your group is large, you may need to limit this to 30 seconds per person.)

A GROUP AGREEMENT (7 minutes)

Most small groups operate with an agreement that includes points such as:

Presence: Attend each meeting unless serious reasons keep you away.

Prayer: Between meeting times, group members pray for one another and for the group's activities together.

Preparation: Group members make the daily readings and exercise a priority, doing them as diligently as life allows.

Participation: Group members will participate honestly and openly in the activities of the sessions.

Confidentiality: What is said within the group remains in the group. Members will not discuss outside the group anything others say within the group.

Courtesy: Group members will listen with respect, without interrupting or engaging in side conversations. When opinions differ, participants will not attempt to persuade others but listen for what God may be saying in the differences.

Display the words *Presence, Prayer, Preparation, Partici-pation, Confidentiality*, and *Courtesy* on newsprint or a board. Mention what each means for this group and ask if folks want to add to or modify these guidelines. Display your group's agreement in the meeting room each time you gather.

INTRODUCING THE STUDY
(8 minutes)

Formational Bible reading. Introduce the study by explaining that *Meeting the Messiah* probably will differ from other Bible studies participants have done. It is based on the principles of formational scripture reading. Direct everyone to the chapter "Reading Scripture Devotionally" (pages 10–15) and point out the main ideas. Ask them to be sure to read this article if they have not already done so. They may use "Informational and Formational Reading" on page 16 as a handy reference throughout the coming weeks as they learn a new way of reading the Bible.

The invitation. Meeting the Messiah invites participants to put themselves in the shoes of different people who prepared for and encountered the Christ child. They will be looking for insight and direction for their own encounter with Jesus during Advent, Christmas, and Epiphany. Each day they will read a short portion of scripture. Then they will read again and look closely at one verse or a few verses from the passage. They will respond to the day's reading by following the process suggested in each *entry point*. Each day's reading and activity will take about ten to fifteen minutes to complete.

The starred entry point. Each week two stars appear beside the title of one of the five entry points. Direct people to page

32, Week 2, Day 1 to show them a starred entry point. Ask group members to make time to do the starred activity each week even if they are unable to do them all, because this starred activity will be part of the weekly group meeting.

The value of journaling. Invite those who already journal to comment briefly about their experience with this practice. Encourage everyone to try journaling in the weeks ahead, and remind them that whatever they write is private, to be shared only if and when they choose.

EXPLORING THE WORD (20 minutes)

THE HOLY SPIRIT

Gather pictures related to the season, such as magazine ads, photos of billboards or shop windows in your area, holiday greeting cards, fliers from stores, holiday event announcements; these may be secular or sacred. You will need at least one picture for each member of the group, preferably a few extra to provide more choices. Prepare a handout with the following questions for each person, or write questions on newsprint or whiteboard prior to the meeting:

- What message does this picture convey about Advent?
- Does this picture stir feelings of desolation or voices of mirth and gladness?
- What is the promise—fulfilled or unfulfilled—that the Holy Spirit yearns for or prompts in you?

Place pictures, cards, advertisements, and other images face down in the center of your gathering space. Ask everyone to turn to Jeremiah 33:10-16 in the Bible or on Day 2 of Week 1. Read together, verse-by-verse around the circle.

Next, ask each person to select one picture from the center along with a question sheet. Give the group several minutes to meditate on the picture in silence and journal their answers on the reverse side of the sheet of paper.

After 10 minutes, invite each person to show his or her picture to the group and briefly share his or her reflections, focusing on the Holy Spirit's prompting through this image.

ENGAGING THE WORD
(*lectio divina*, 40-45 minutes)

1 Corinthians 2:9-12.
Before beginning *lectio divina*, remind the group that everyone responds differently to scripture and that whatever they experience will be fine. Ask for a volunteer to read on the third hearing and direct participants to sit in groups of three.

Refer to the guide for leading *lectio divina* (pages 97–99). Announce and post the reference (Bible chapter and verse) of the passage the group will be hearing, and remind them that they are to listen, not to read along in the Bible, and that you will lead them through the process.

After *lectio divina*, request one or two minutes of silence to allow people to make notes about what they heard.

CLOSING (10 minutes)

First, ask if anyone would like to volunteer to create/arrange the worship center for upcoming sessions. Then ask for a volunteer to choose and lead music for the sessions.

Second, explain that each participant will be invited to develop and experiment with a *breath prayer* throughout the season of Advent. Based on the command in 1 Thessalonians

5:17 to "pray without ceasing," the breath prayer is a six- to eight-syllable prayer that matches the rhythm of inhaling and exhaling. With practice, one becomes able to pray as naturally as one breathes.

Ask group members to get comfortable, relax, and close their eyes. Invite them each to choose a name for God that is most meaningful to him or her, such as, *Holy God, Father, Mother, God-with-Us.* After a minute, instruct participants to be in prayer about what they most desire this Advent season, whether it be to experience Christ anew, to be present to family, a sense of peace, or another specific yearning. After a couple minutes of silent prayer, ask each person to form his or her unique breath prayer as follows. The aim is a six- to eight-syllable prayer.

1. Express their desire in a short phrase.

2. Add their chosen name for God to that deep desire to form the prayer. For example, *God with Us, calm my soul.*

When everyone has discerned his or her breath prayer, allow three minutes of silence to pray without ceasing. Say, **Breathing in, say the name of God. Breathing out, say your desire.** After the silence, close with the words, **And all God's people said . . .** To which the group can respond, **Amen.**

Encourage participants to live with this prayer each day, beginning their devotional time with the prayer and coming back to it throughout the day.

Session 2

John the Baptist

Assemble materials: preprinted questions for Interacting with the Word; paper, pens, and pencils

Note: All meeting outlines are for 90-minute sessions; if you are using this study in a 45-minute session, omit the *lectio divina* experience (Engaging the Word).

OPENING PRAYER (5 minutes)

Light the Christ candle and remind the group that we light the candle not to bring God into our midst but to recognize that God is already present with us. Welcome people back and review the group agreement: Presence, Prayer, Preparation, Participation, Confidentiality, and Courtesy.

Invite the music leader to lead a song. Then pray this prayer or one of your own:

> Holy God, as you anointed John to prepare the way for Jesus, prepare our hearts to receive the Good News of your Son. Open our hearts to the blessing of his presence and open our minds to the challenge of his call on our lives. Amen.

INTERACTING WITH THE WORD
(15 minutes)

Invite group members to sit in groups of two or three persons. Give them a couple minutes to review their responses to the week's scripture experiences.

The following are several questions the smaller groups

(triads) might use when discussing each week's Bible reading and responses. Choose two questions—and others you wish to add—for the discussion this week and gauge the group's response to them. You may use the same questions each week or vary them. Write the questions you'll be using on a board or flip chart. Encourage group members to listen for God in each person's words. Remind everyone to allow each group member time to respond to a question before the group moves on to the next.

- What scripture passage from the past week do you remember as especially meaningful, and why?
- Which daily exercise did you most enjoy, and which was the most difficult for you?
- How did the daily readings connect to what has been going on in your life this week? Was one especially appropriate? If so, in what way?
- Which exercise surprised you or helped you realize something about yourself?
- How did the daily readings cause you to change a behavior?
- What do you want to remember from this week's readings, and why?

EXPLORING THE WORD (20 minutes)

This activity builds on the entry point for Luke 3:7-18.

Pass out paper and pens or pencils. Ask participants to get out their calendars (electronic or paper) or to-do lists if they have them stashed in their pockets or purses. Then ask each person to review these lists (or those unwritten lists in their minds) and write down his or her Christmas to-do list on the paper. A list might have activities like bake cookies, plan office party, buy presents, make costume for Christmas pageant, write check to favorite charity, clean for guests, daily devotions, and so on. Give the group three or four minutes to write out lists.

Ask for volunteers to describe what it felt like to make the list. Was it comforting to get it on paper? overwhelming? Did it bring relief or stress? Discuss for five minutes.

Next, ask someone to read Luke 3:7-18. Then have the group form pairs and look at each other's lists together. Have the pairs imagine going to John with their lists and asking, "What should we do?" (vv. 10, 12, 14). Have them talk together for five minutes about how John might respond.

In the closing minutes, ask each person to take back his or her list and prayerfully remove items from the to-do list or add preparations that might better reflect the spirit of Advent.

ALTERNATE CLOSING ACTIVITY

Invite people to turn over their to-do list. On the back, they can rewrite Luke 3:7-18 as if it were John's exhortation to each of them personally. If they could ask, *What should we do to prepare for Jesus' coming?* how would John respond?

ENGAGING THE WORD
(*lectio divina*, 45 minutes)

Ask for a volunteer to read on the third hearing and direct participants to sit in groups of three. Use the steps outlined for leading group *lectio* to guide the group through contemplation of Isaiah 35:8-10. After *lectio divina*, ask for one or two minutes of silence to allow those who wish to make notes.

CLOSING (5 minutes)

Ask if anyone practiced the breath prayer this week. If so, ask for brief comments about how that influenced his or her experience of Advent. Encourage participants to continue this week with the same breath prayer or to modify it based on their experience during the session.

Invite the music leader to lead the group in a song.

Invite special concerns that group members want to pray about now and in the coming week. Then pray this prayer or one of your own, mentioning the group's concerns at the end:

> God of Grace, we come to this Advent with the same expectation and questioning of those who first came to John the Baptist. May we have the courage to rethink Advent this year, embracing the preparations that will sustain us during this blessed season. Amen.

Extinguish the candle and say, **Go into the world to proclaim the good news to the people.**

Session 3

Mary

Assemble materials: preprinted questions for Interacting with the Word; a large picture of Mary (in an art book, a painting in your church, an icon, or a picture printed from the Internet); newsprint and markers

Note: The candle-lighting prayer for this session is one used in the traditional praying of the Rosary, a Catholic prayer tradition. The word *rosary* derives from a Latin word meaning a garden of roses, the rose being one of the flowers used to symbolize the Virgin Mary. The Rosary consists of a set number of specific prayers. First are the introductory prayers: one Apostles' Creed (Credo), one Our Father (the Lord's Prayer), three Hail Marys, one Glory Be (Gloria Patri). After Vatican II, the Rosary was used less often, but in recent years it has regained popularity, and many Protestants now say the Rosary, recognizing it as a truly biblical form of prayer.

The prayer below is traditionally known as the Hail Mary. It begins, "Hail Mary, full of grace, the Lord is with thee." This is the greeting the angel Gabriel gave Mary in Luke 1:28 (Confraternity Version). The next part reads, "Blessed art thou among women, and blessed is the fruit of thy womb, Jesus." This is what Mary's cousin Elizabeth said to her in Luke 1:42. The only additions to these two verses are the names *Jesus* and *Mary*, to make clear who is being referred to.

OPENING PRAYER (10 minutes)

Light the Christ candle, saying, **We light the candle and recite the words of the Catholic Rosary prayer, based on Luke 1:28, 42: "Hail Mary, full of grace, the Lord is with you! Blessed are you among women, and blessed is the fruit of your womb, Jesus."**

Or you may pray the opening line from Mary's Song of Praise in Luke 1:46: **"My soul magnifies the Lord, and my spirit rejoices in God my Savior."**

Invite the music leader to help the group sing a song.

Bring a picture of the Virgin Mary. Invite the group

simply to gaze at the image in silence, imagining this young woman's calling and obedience to serve as the God-bearer for the Son of God. After several minutes, invite each person to name aloud an adjective that describes Mary. Then close with this prayer:

> God of our Salvation, enable us to trust as Mary did, to hear the word of peace in the face of our fears, and to give our lives over to you in joyful obedience. Amen.

INTERACTING WITH THE WORD
(15 minutes)

Divide the group into threes. Begin by allowing a couple minutes for them to review their responses to the daily readings. Choose two questions from those on page 107 and others you may want to add for discussion this week. Write the questions you'll be using on a board or flip chart. Encourage group members to listen for God in each person's words. Remind everyone to allow each group member time to respond to a question before the group moves on to the next.

EXPLORING THE WORD (20 minutes)

This activity builds on Isaiah 12:2-6.

Divide participants into three groups. Assign each group one of these passages: Jeremiah 1:4-8; 15: 15-21; Jonah 1:1–3:3; Luke 1:26-38. If your group is larger, have two or three groups looking at each of the three scriptures.

Pass out a sheet of newsprint and a set of markers to each group. Ask groups to read the assigned passage and to discuss the following questions (post these on newsprint):

- How did the person in this passage hear the call of God?
- How did each person respond initially?
- How was God present with him/her?
- How did he/she come to obedience?

After people have discussed the story, invite them to depict the person's call and obedience on the newsprint. It could be in an image, a flow chart, a summary, a song, or any other kind of representation they think of. Allow time for each group to present their work to the larger group.

If there is time, invite people to choose the character that each most identifies with this Advent. Give everyone a piece of paper and pen; direct them to create two columns. Put their name above the left-hand column and the Bible character's name above the right-hand column. Explain that they will engage in a prayerful and imaginative dialogue with the character: **Begin by writing a question to the character in the left-hand column. Consider how that person might reply and write the response in the right-hand column. Continue this conversation for several minutes.**

Close with a silent prayer of thanksgiving or commitment.

ENGAGING THE WORD
(*lectio divina*, 45 minutes)

Ask for a volunteer to read on the third hearing and direct participants to sit in groups of three. Use the steps outlined for guiding group *lectio* to guide the group through contemplation of Luke 1:26-30. After *lectio divina*, request silence to allow those who wish to make notes about what they heard.

CLOSING (5 minutes)

Ask who has practiced the breath prayer this week and how that is affecting their experience of Advent. Encourage participants to continue this week with the same breath prayer or to modify based on their experience during the session.

Invite the music leader to lead the group in a song.

Invite concerns to pray about now and in the coming week. Then pray Mary's Song of Praise from Luke 1:46-55:

> My soul magnifies the Lord,
>> and my spirit rejoices in God my Savior,
> for he has looked with favor on the lowliness of his
>> servant.
> Surely, from now on all generations will call me blessed;
> for the Mighty One has done great things for me,
>> and holy is his name.
> His mercy is for those who fear him
>> from generation to generation.
> He has shown strength with his arm;
>> he has scattered the proud in the thoughts of their
>> hearts.
> He has brought down the powerful from their thrones,
>> and lifted up the lowly;
> he has filled the hungry with good things,
>> and sent the rich away empty.
> He has helped his servant Israel,
>> in remembrance of his mercy,
> according to the promise he made to our ancestors,
>> to Abraham and to his descendants forever.

Session 4
The Shepherds

Assemble materials: Luke 2:14 prewritten for display; prewritten questions for Interacting with the Word; handout for Exploring the Word, clay pots, permanent markers, paper strips, cotton balls

OPENING (5 minutes)

Before the group arrives, write Luke 2:14 on newsprint or whiteboard:

> Glory to God in the highest heaven,
>   and on earth peace among those whom he favors!

Begin by dividing the group in half. Ask one half to read "Glory to God in the highest heaven" and the second half to respond, "and on earth peace among those whom he favors." Pray this verse responsively three to five times, allowing the Spirit to prompt your ending. At the close of this prayer, light the Christ candle, praying one final time in unison,

> Glory to God in the highest heaven,
>   and on earth peace among those whom he favors!

Ask the music leader to lead the group in a song.

INTERACTING WITH THE WORD
(15 minutes)

Invite participants to sit in groups of two or three persons. Allow a couple minutes for them to review their responses to the daily readings.

Use the questions on page 107 and others you may create for discussion starters in the small groups. Write the questions you'll be using on a board or flip chart. Encourage group members to listen for God in each person's words. Remind everyone to allow each group member time to respond to a question before the group moves on to the next.

EXPLORING THE WORD (20 minutes)

This activity builds on Psalm 96.

Ask for a volunteer to read 2 Corinthians 4:7-16.

Use this introduction or something similar: **If we were to choose the most effective and deserving individuals to proclaim the good news—to bear witness to the light of Jesus in the world—a group of ragtag, lowly, dirty shepherds on the edges of town would hardly be our first choice. But God often chooses those who are broken and vulnerable as messengers of God's greatest glory and good news. Today we will take time to consider how the cracks in our own lives allow God's glory to shine through.**

In advance, print up a handout with the following list of scripture passages, instructions, and final reflection questions to distribute to each person, or write this information on newsprint or whiteboard that everyone can see. Give each person a Bible and a four-inch clay pot (available at most hardware or home improvement stores). Provide a supply of permanent markers in several colors and a pile of small paper strips.

Read Psalm 139:13-16: Draw on the pot to depict or represent your physical characteristics. Using a colored marker, write on the pot qualities by which people know you.

Read Genesis 1:26-27, 31: Choose a different color marker; on the outside of the pot, write characteristics of yours that reflect God's image.

Read Proverbs 26:18-23. How do you try to gloss over certain parts of yourself? What bravado or false self do you project to the world? Find a way to represent this "glaze" on your pot.

Read Romans 9:20-24. What don't you like about yourself? What would you change that God has created in you? Illustrate or describe these desires on your pot.

Read 2 Corinthians 4:5-12. What treasure do you carry on the inside? Write these gifts, abilities, and treasures on strips of paper and place them inside your pot.

Final Reflection Questions:

How does the light of Christ—through your gifts and abilities— shine out from even your darkness and brokenness?

When has your affliction, questioning, or persecution made Jesus visible to those around you?

Ask everyone to work on his or her pot quietly and prayerfully. Allow time for sharing, either one-on-one or in the group. Participants who volunteer may explain their pot to one other person or share with the group.

ENGAGING THE WORD
(*lectio divina*, 45 minutes)

Ask for a volunteer to read on the third hearing and direct participants to sit in groups of three. Using the steps for *lectio divina*, guide the group through contemplation of 1 Peter 3:15-17.

After *lectio divina*, ask for one or two minutes of silence to allow those who wish to make notes.

CLOSING (5 minutes)

Invite people to share their experiences of using breath prayer this week. Encourage participants to continue this week with the same breath prayer or to modify based on their experience during the session.

Have the music volunteer lead the group in a song.

Ask if there are special concerns that group members want to pray about now and in the coming week.

Hand a cotton ball to each participant as a reminder of the shepherds' lowly position as well as their privileged position as God's messengers of good news. Suggest participants add the cotton to their flowerpots.

Extinguish the candle and pray,

Lord, may we go forward aware of both our gifts and our weaknesses, glorifying and praising your name, as witnesses to the Light. Amen.

Session 5
Jesus

Assemble materials: barbed-wire candle for Opening and Closing, votive candles (one for each participant); predrawn diagram for Exploring the Word; prewritten questions for Interacting with the Word

OPENING (10 minutes)

For this session a special candle will enhance the theme. A simple white candle with a strand of barbed wire coiled around it is the symbol of Amnesty International and also of the South African struggle to bring down apartheid. (See http://www.pbase.com/eastkent64/image/101995467 for an image.) You can create your own by placing a barbed wire or other wire mesh around a candle. You can create a similar effect by setting a candle in modeling clay or Play-Doh, making a wide enough clay perimeter around the candle to erect toothpicks, knives, or forks; these represent the boundary and danger implied by barbed wire.

Read aloud John 1:1-5 and light the special candle as you finish reading.

Share some background about the barbed-wire candle and its significance in the struggle against apartheid. Amnesty International's founder, Peter Benenson, asked artist Diana Redhouse to design an emblem for the organization. He had thought of a candle encircled in barbed wire when recalling the proverb *Better to light a candle than curse the darkness.*

That candle now symbolizes the organization's goals: shining the light of public attention on abuses perpetrated by human rights violators; being a spark for positive change; creating a beacon of hope and solidarity for those who defend human rights at great personal risk and for people jailed, tortured, "disappeared," or forced to become refugees.[6]

A similar candle played a role in South Africa's history, when those opposed to the apartheid regime were disappearing and being killed. Each day, persons would gather to light a candle and read the names of those who had disappeared since the last lighting. This simple act—lighting the candle in the midst of the dark days and remembering those who had fought for justice—spoke truth, love, and light to power.

Conclude by saying, **Lighting the candle today, as we celebrate Christ's birth, reminds us that as Christians, we do not deny the darkness but celebrate the light that shines in the midst of the darkness, whether in our personal lives or the greater world.**

Ask the music leader to lead the group in a song.

INTERACTING WITH THE WORD
(15 minutes)

Invite people to sit in groups of two or three persons. Allow time to review responses to the daily readings. They may use the questions on page 107 or others you have created in previous weeks. Encourage listening for God in one another's words. Remind everyone to allow each group member time to respond.

EXPLORING THE WORD (20 minutes)

This activity builds on Hebrews 1:1-4.

Explain that you will lead the group in a guided meditation on the power of God's light in Christ, how we are changed when that light is present in us.

Read the following meditation slowly, purposefully, and with pauses for reflection where the ellipses appear: **Get as comfortable as you can within our space. Close your eyes if you wish, and take three deep breaths to center yourself . . . . As you hear different places or communities named and described, try to use all of your senses to imagine them** with as much detail as you can. Notice how you feel, what sounds you hear, what you see directly and in the periphery of your imagination. And be especially attuned to the places of darkness and light. . . .

[During this pause, dim or turn out the lights except for the candle at the center of your gathering space.]

Take another deep breath and imagine standing outside your house, apartment, or dormitory. . . . As you stand and look at your home, call to mind the different people who have or will enter there during the Christmas season. . . . Where is the light of Christ in your home? . . . Where is there darkness? . . . What conflicts or tensions, like barbed wire, threaten the light in your home or in your relationships? . . . Who *bears* that light in your home? How? . . . In your imagination, now walk through your home's interior, carrying the light of Christ into each space and room, offering the light to each person you meet. . . .

Now imagine yourself at your workplace or another daily destination, maybe a classroom, your child's school, a favorite coffee shop, or a shopping mall. . . . Imagine entering this place as if for the first time. Do not look with human eyes, but look at the place and the people through the eyes of Jesus, the true light that enlightens everyone. . . . Where do you sense the light of Christ breaking in? How are people drawn to the light? . . . Who or what surrounds the light that intimidates or repels people from the light of Christ? . . . What would it look like for you to bear witness to the light of Christ in this place? . . . Let that scene unfold before your mind's eye. . . .

Next, imagine going to your church. . . . As you walk or

drive toward your church, notice the darkness in the community around your church. . . . Who is despairing? What situations in your community seem hopeless? . . . Where do you sense an absence of God? . . . As you draw nearer to the church, imagine a bright light shining brilliantly from the inside out—through the doors, windows, cracks, and crevices. . . . Where do you see the light of Christ in your congregation? . . . How are you called to take that light into the hurting and dark world beyond the church? . . . Imagine the rays of light from the church touching the darkest places that you have passed on your way in. . . . What transformation is possible? . . .

Bring your thoughts back to this time and this gathering. We remember that we are not the light but only bear witness to the light. So take a few moments to rest in the presence of God . . . in the Word . . . in the life that is a light of all people.

Invite participants, as they are ready, to open their eyes. Ask for volunteers to share any insights, reactions, or reflections on this guided meditation. You may ask the question, **Where, or in whom, is Jesus' presence made real this Christmas?**

ENGAGING THE WORD
(*lectio divina*, 45 minutes)

Ask for a volunteer to read on the third hearing and direct participants to sit in groups of three. Use the steps outlined for leading group *lectio* to guide the group through contemplation of John 14:8-11. After *lectio divina*, ask for one or two minutes of silence to allow people to make notes.

CLOSING (5 minutes)

Ask about practice of the breath prayer. How is it influencing people's experience of Christmas? Encourage participants to continue this week with the same breath prayer or to modify based on their experience during the session.

Invite concerns that group members want to pray about now and in the coming week.

Distribute a votive candle to each person. Form a circle around the table with the special candle. Ask for a volunteer to begin a candle-lighting ceremony.

That first person lights his or her candle from the central candle, then says to the person on the right, "The light shines in the darkness, and the darkness did not overcome it." That individual tilts her or his candle into the flame of the first person's candle to receive the flame. Continue around the circle until each person is holding a lit candle.

Invite the music leader to lead the group in a song.

Turn the lights back on and send the group forth with the words of Isaiah 9:6-7:

> **For a child has been born for us,**
> **a son given to us;**
> **authority rests upon his shoulders,**
> **and he is named**
> **Wonderful Counselor, Mighty God,**
> **Everlasting Father, Prince of Peace.**
> **His authority shall grow continually,**
> **and there shall be endless peace**
> **for the throne of David and his kingdom.**
> **He will establish and uphold it**
> **with justice and with righteousness**

from this time onward and forevermore.
The zeal of the LORD of hosts will do this.
Amen.

Session 6

The Magi

Assemble materials: prewritten questions for Interacting with the Word and Exploring the Word

OPENING (5 minutes)

Begin with these words:

The Psalms of Ascent, or the Pilgrim Psalms, were written to remember the journey to Jerusalem for feast days. Traveling together, these early pilgrims sought to experience and celebrate the presence of God, just as the wise men traveled together to meet and worship the Christ child.

Let us stand and greet one another as fellow pilgrims embracing and saying,

"Peace be with you."

"And also with you."

Motion for everyone to be seated. Then light the Christ candle, saying, **We recognize the light of Christ in our midst and in the lives of those we travel with this Advent. Amen.**

INTERACTING WITH THE WORD
(15 minutes)

Invite participants to sit in groups of two or three persons to share responses to the daily readings. Use the questions on page 107 or others that work well for your group. Encourage people to listen for God in each person's words and allow each person time to respond.

EXPLORING THE WORD (20 minutes)

This activity builds on Deuteronomy 8:1-20.

The wise men, or Magi, visited Jesus, bearing gifts. Renowned for expertise in astrology, these men (traditionally assumed to be the three in number because of the three gifts) followed a star to Jesus' location. There they bowed down and worshiped him, returning another way to avoid King Herod.

Say, **As we heard in the Opening Prayer, the wise men were not the first to set out on long and arduous journeys. Our tradition is full of pilgrims who set out based on their beliefs, trusting in God's presence and inspired by hope. Let's look at a couple of these journeys.**

Direct attention to the diagram you have prepared.

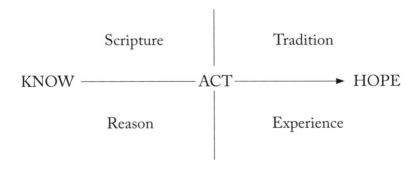

Explain that the arrow across the center of the page represents the journey of faith—the pilgrimage—that all believers are called to make. The four quadrants represent the way we make sense of our journeys through a mingling of **scripture**, religious **tradition**, intellectual **reason**, and personal **experience**. (In the Wesleyan tradition, this concept is called the Wesleyan Quadrilateral.) The group will look at three different journeys in light of this diagram.

First, read together Deuteronomy 8:1-20. Ask for volunteers to name those things that the Israelites "know" that allow them to act and to hope. As persons make their responses, note how this knowledge comes to the Israelites: by tradition or by experience? Next, discuss together how someone's story (history) impacts the present. Similarly, how does someone's hope for the future impact current decisions?

Next, direct persons to find a partner. Give each pair a sheet of paper and pen. Ask them to read Matthew 2:1-12, and then draw a similar diagram to understand the pilgrimage the Magi made.

Finally, give everyone paper and pen. Now participants will consider their own life in light of this grid. Give the group five minutes to journal in response to the following questions (write them on newsprint for everyone to see):

- What knowledge or experience marks the beginning of your pilgrimage?
- How have your history and belief informed your present actions or decisions?
- After your journey to meet the Messiah this Advent, Christmas, and Epiphany, what is your hope as you go

forward? How is that hope informed by scripture, tradition, reason, and experience?

ENGAGING THE WORD
(lectio divina, 45 minutes)

Ask for a volunteer to read on the third hearing and direct participants to sit in groups of three. Guide the group in the contemplation of Isaiah 43:15-19. After *lectio divina*, ask for a short silence to allow those who wish to make notes.

CLOSING (5 minutes)

Invite participants who are willing to share their experience with the breath prayer during Advent, Christmas, and Epiphany. Do any feel their breath prayer has been answered? What gifts have any received in prayer during this time?

Ask for special concerns that group members want to pray about now and in the coming week.

Say, **The Magi came to Jesus, the Messiah, to worship him and offer him their gifts. As we close our reflection on this journey through Advent, Christmas, and Epiphany, what gift do you wish to offer to the Christ child? Take a few moments to think of or write down a prayer of offering to Jesus, giving thanks for his presence or acknowledging your hope for the future.**

After a minute of silence, ask each person to pray aloud his or her offering prayer. Close by singing together:

> **Praise God from whom all blessings flow;**
> **praise God, all creatures here below;**
> **praise God above, ye heavenly host,**
> **praise Father, Son, and Holy Ghost. Amen.**

NOTES

1. *The Interior Castle* (West Valley City, UT: Waking Lion Press/Editorium, 2006), 22.

2. *The Sacrament of the Present Moment*, trans. Kitty Muggeridge (New York: HarperCollins, 1989), 91.

3. *Encounter with God's Love: Selected Writings of Julian of Norwich*, ed. Keith Beasley-Topliffe (Nashville: Upper Room Books, 1998), 50, 53.

4. *African Bible Commentary*, ed. Tokunboh Adeyemo (Word Alive Publishers / Zondervan, 2006), 1208.

5. Jan van Ruysbroek, *The Spiritual Espousals*, trans. Eric Colledge (New York: Harper & Brothers, n.d.), 127–28.

6. http://www.amnesty.ca/about/history/history_of_ amnesty_international/meaning_of_the_Amnesty_ candle.php